# The Most Powerful Storm on Earth

### by Linda Cernak

**Scott Foresman**
is an imprint of

Glenview, Illinois • Boston, Massachusetts • Chandler, Arizona •
Upper Saddle River, New Jersey

**Photographs**

Every effort has been made to secure permission and provide appropriate credit for photographic material. The publisher deeply regrets any omission and pledges to correct errors called to its attention in subsequent editions.

Unless otherwise acknowledged, all photographs are the property of Pearson Education, Inc.

Photo locators denoted as follows: Top (T), Center (C), Bottom (B), Left (L), Right (R), Background (Bkgd)

**Opener** ©A. T. Willett/Alamy; **1** (T) ©A. T. Willett/Alamy, (B) ©Alexey Stiop/Shutterstock; **3** ©A. T. Willett/Alamy; **4** ©A. T. Willett/Alamy; **5** ©Jason Politte/Alamy; **8** ©Alexey Stiop/Shutterstock; **9**. ©Jupiter Images/Comstock Images/Alamy; **10** ©Ryan McGinnis/Alamy; **11** ©Dennis M. Sabangan/Corbis; **12** ©Steve Jaffe/AFP/Getty Images.

ISBN 13: 978-0-328-47243-7
ISBN 10:   0-328-47243-3

9 10 V010 13

The sky is a stormy gray. Rain pours down. Lightning flashes and thunder booms. You hear a loud roar that sounds like a train. What could it be?

It's a tornado! A tornado is the most powerful storm on Earth. It's a spinning funnel of air.

The funnel comes from the storm clouds above. Warm air fights with cool air. Wet air fights with dry air. High winds push everything around. The funnel moves faster and faster.

spinning storm

storm funnel

Tornadoes are hard to predict. They take shape and travel very quickly. There's little time to warn people that one is coming.

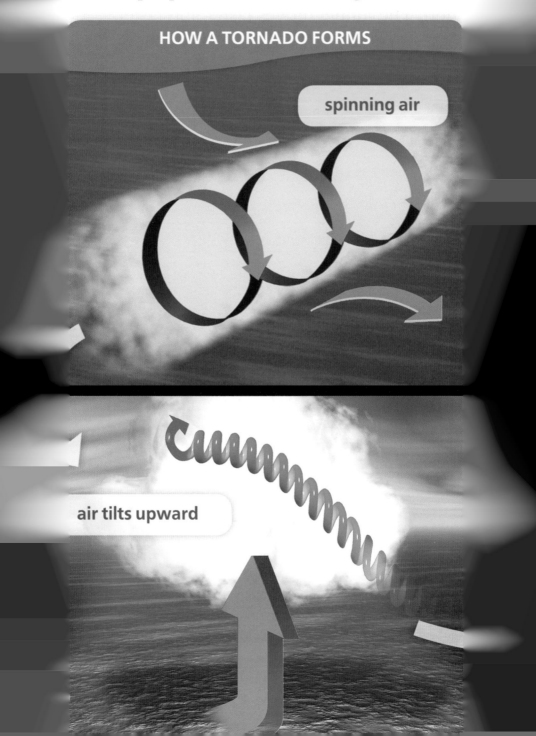

HOW A TORNADO FORMS

spinning air

air tilts upward

It's also hard to predict a tornado's path. rnadoes can travel in random paths for one or o miles.

funnel cloud

The strongest tornadoes have wind speeds of more than 300 miles per hour! Houses are blown to bits and cars are tossed in the air. Trees are pulled out of the ground.

Every state in the United States has tornadoes. But most tornadoes happen in the Midwest. This area is called Tornado Alley.

Tornado Alley

North Dakota

South Dakota

Nebraska

Iowa

Colorado

Kansas

Missouri

Oklahoma

Arkansas

Texas

What should you do if you hear a tornado warning? First, get inside right away. Go to the basement if you have one.

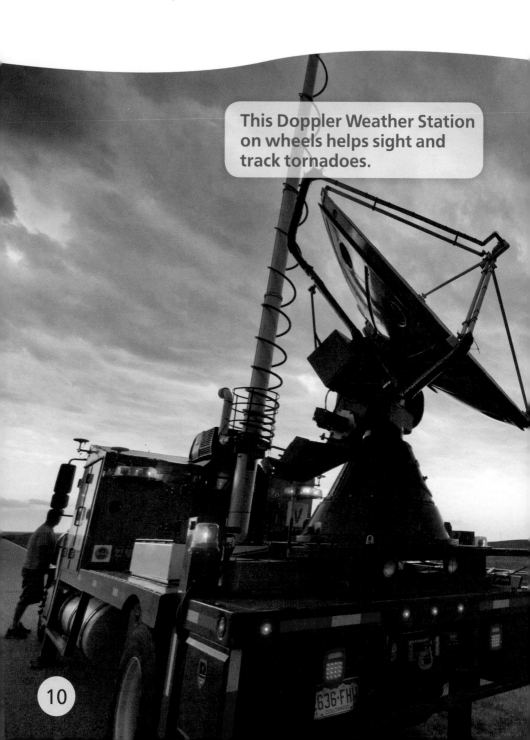

This Doppler Weather Station on wheels helps sight and track tornadoes.

If you don't have a basement, stay away from windows. Go under a stairway or a heavy table. Cover yourself with a mattress or heavy blankets.

A tornado may be over in minutes, even seconds. But it can do terrible things in that time. It is, after all, the most powerful storm on Earth.